ABRAHAM

Friedel Steinmann and Werner Steinmann

Scripture Union
130 City Road, London EC1V 2NJ

© 1988 Friedel Steinmann und Werner Steinmann
Theologischer Verlag GbR, Hamburg
First published by Steinmann & Steinmann as *Abraham oder der Weg hinauf nach Morija*

Translation by Elrose Hunter and Simon Jenkins
First English edition 1989

ISBN 0 86201 612 6

Printed and bound in Great Britain by Cox and Wyman Ltd, Reading

Right from the beginning, God has had a lot to do with us human beings. He made us and showed us his love in many different ways. He gave the first people the freedom to explore the earth and to use it wisely. But they turned away from God and foolishly went off in the opposite direction. That could have been the end of the story. But because God doesn't give up easily, it was only the beginning . . .

A LONG LONG TIME AGO, THERE LIVED IN THE WILDS OF THE ARABIAN DESERT A SMALL TRIBE OF NOMADS...

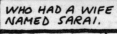

7

IT TOOK TWENTY YEARS FOR ALL THE PREPARATIONS.

NAHOR TRIED A FEW TIMES TO PERSUADE HIM TO STAY...

AT LAST THEY WERE READY.

THERE'S JUST TOO MUCH!

ABRAM! I'VE FINISHED PACKING!

♪ THE LONG AND WINDING ROAD... ♫♪

SIGH... WILL WE EVER SEE EACH OTHER AGAIN?

MANY WEEKS LATER...

WELL, THIS IS IT. CANAAN!

SO! WHAT HAPPENS NEXT?

YEAH. WHAT NOW?

SEARCH ME!

THAT NIGHT, NEAR SHEC (AT THE OAK OF MOREH)

BUT GOD PUNISHED PHARAOH AND HIS HOUSEHOLD WITH SEVERE PLAGUES BECAUSE HE HAD TAKEN SARAI INTO HIS HOUSE.

27

SO ABRAM LEFT EGYPT A MUCH RICHER MAN.

ABRAM AND LOT SPENT A LONG TIME WANDERING AROUND. FINALLY THEY REACHED THE JORDAN VALLEY.

BOTH OF THEM HAD LARGE FLOCKS AND MANY HERDSMEN...

HEY! KINDLY TAKE YOUR ANIMALS SOMEWHERE ELSE!

... WHO WERE RATHER IRRITABLE AFTER THE LONG JOURNEY.

WE WERE HERE FIRST!

NO! WE WERE!

CUT IT OUT!

ONE DAY —

ABRAM, I'M TOO OLD TO HAVE CHILDREN...

...TAKE MY MAID, HAGAR!

WHAT?

IS THAT WHAT GOD MEANT?

THERE'S NO OTHER WAY YOU'LL HAVE A SON!

HAGAR BECAME PREGNANT AND GAVE ABRAM A SON: ISHMAEL.

13 YEARS LATER, WHEN ABRAM WAS CELEBRATING HIS 99TH BIRTHDAY, GOD SPOKE TO HIM AGAIN.
ABRAM! FROM NOW ON YOUR NAME IS ABRAHAM AND YOUR WIFE WILL BE CALLED SARAH!
FOR HE'S A JOLLY GOOD FELLOW...
CHEERS!

37

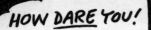

50

TAKING THE ANGEL'S ADVICE, NONE OF THEM LOOKED BACK, EXCEPT LOT'S WIFE...

SHE BECAME A PILLAR OF SALT.

53

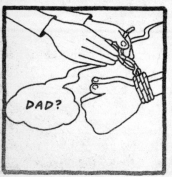

The story ends here. We don't know whether Isaac asked his father any more questions or if he did, how Abraham answered him. We don't know whether Abraham talked to his wife or to Lot about what happened on the mountain. But we do know this. Abraham's descendants went on to become a great nation, just as God had promised. And one of his descendants – a man named Jesus – has brought God's blessing and happiness to the whole world.

Whenever someone puts their life into God's hands (as Abraham did) they too can receive the happiness God has promised.